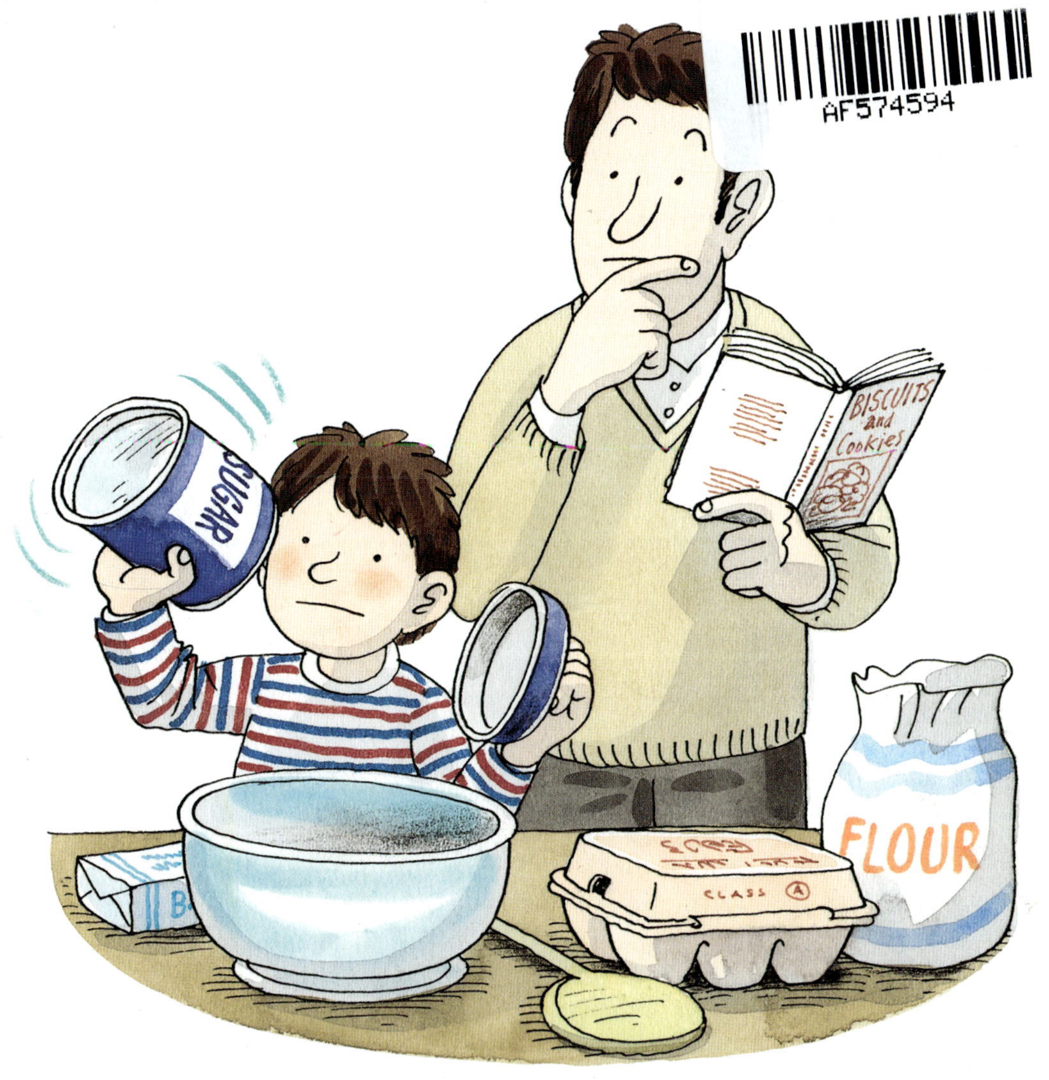

Chip wanted some sugar.

He went to the supermarket.

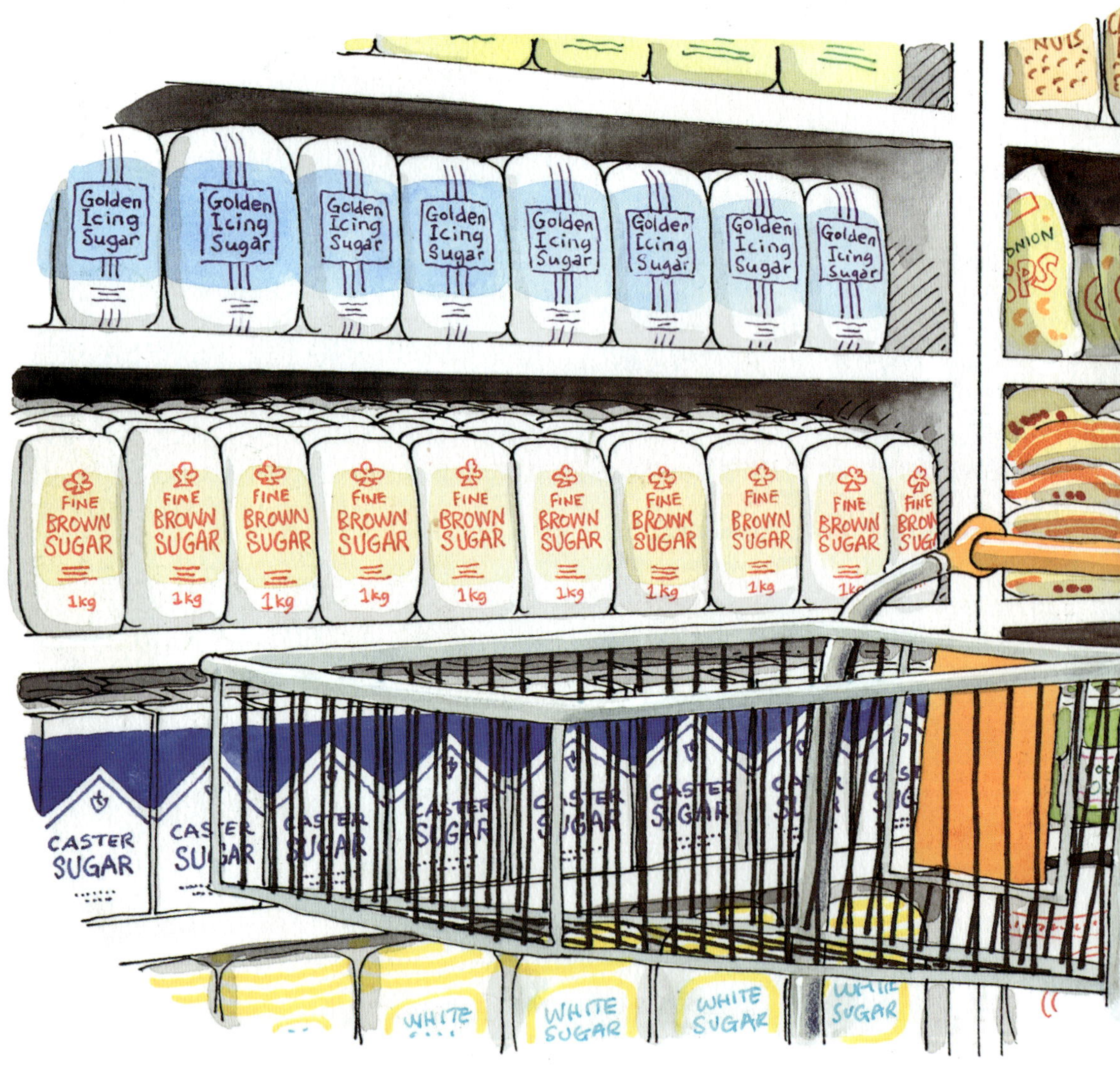

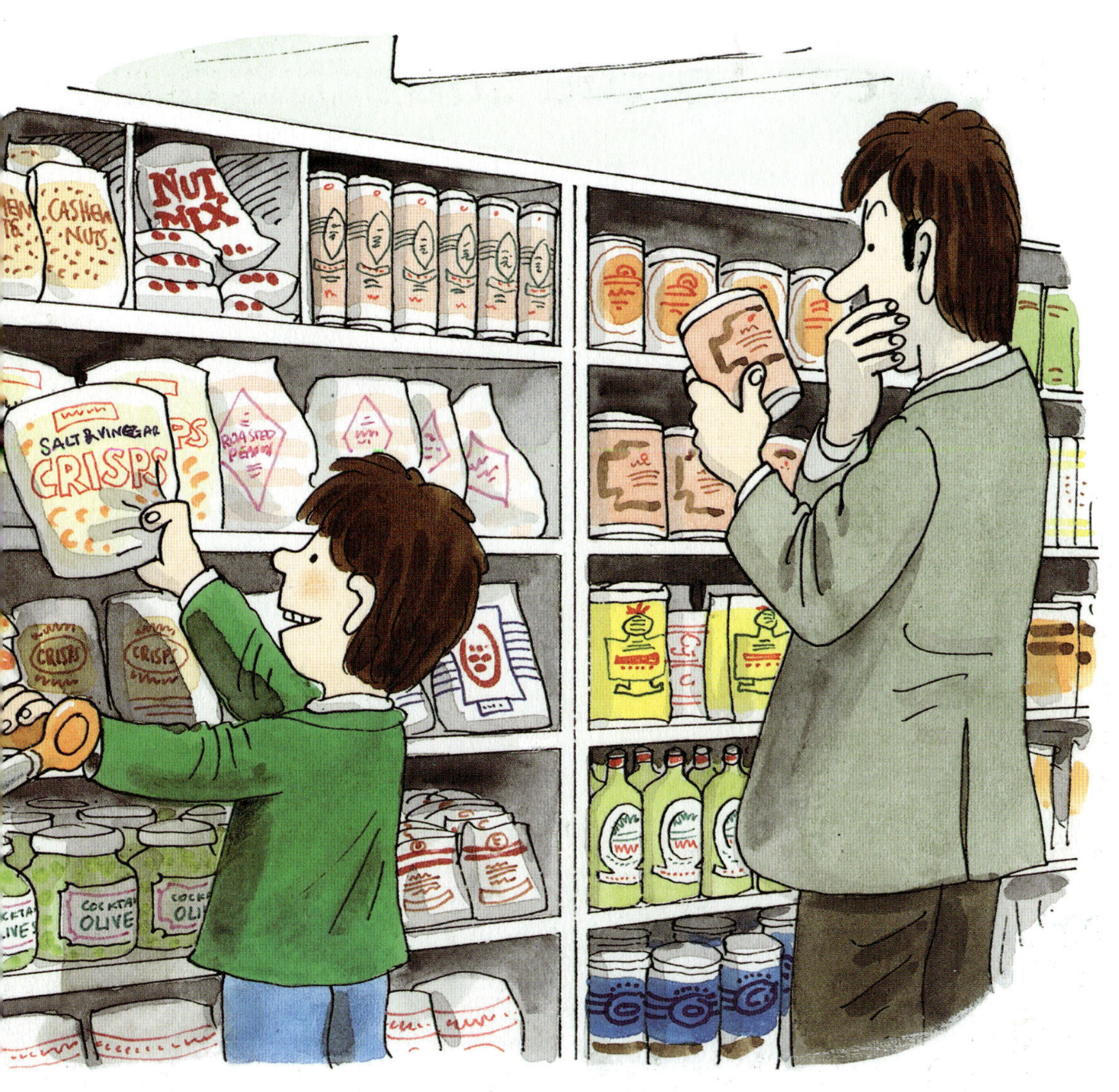

He got some crisps.

He went to the shop.

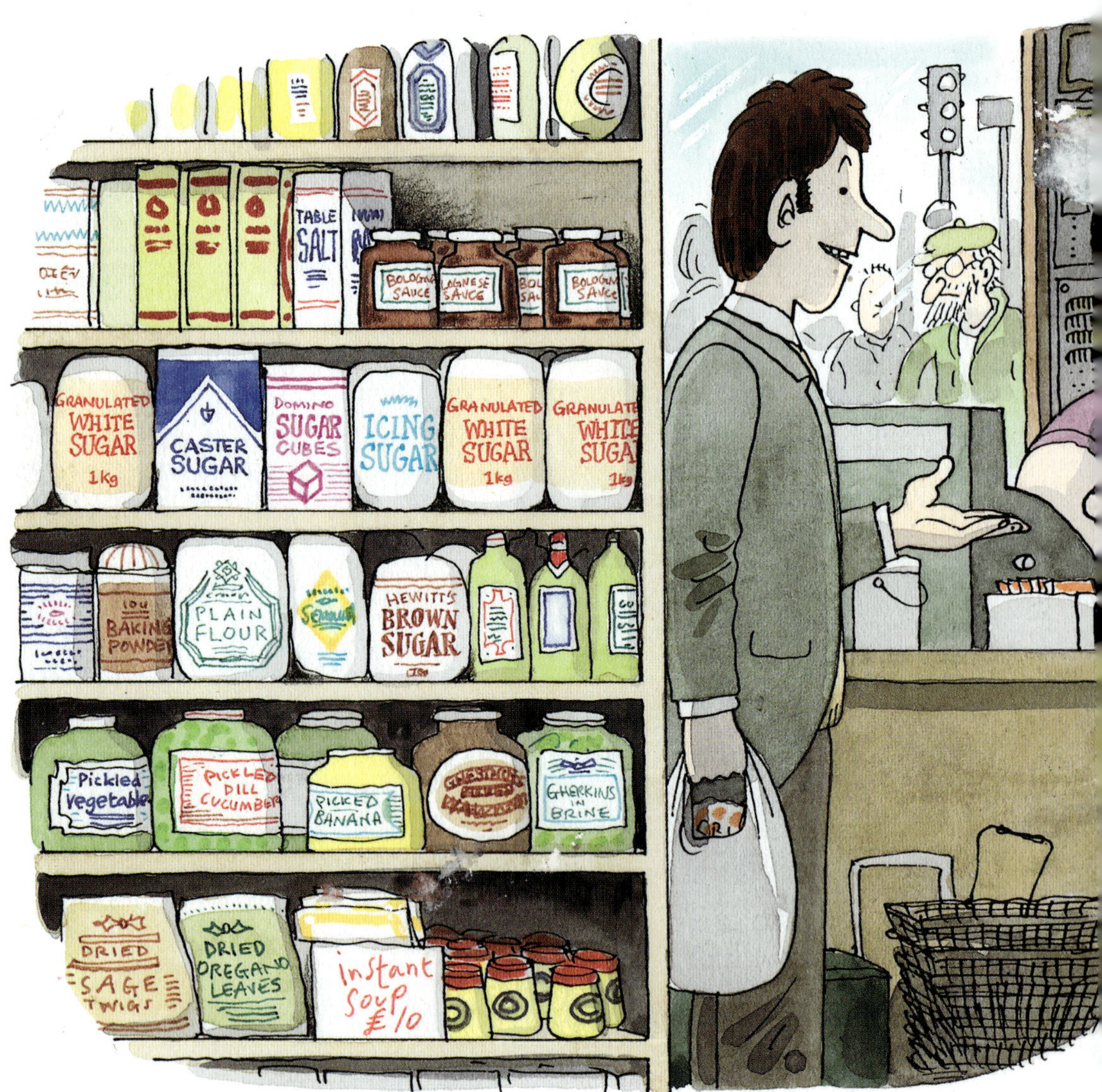

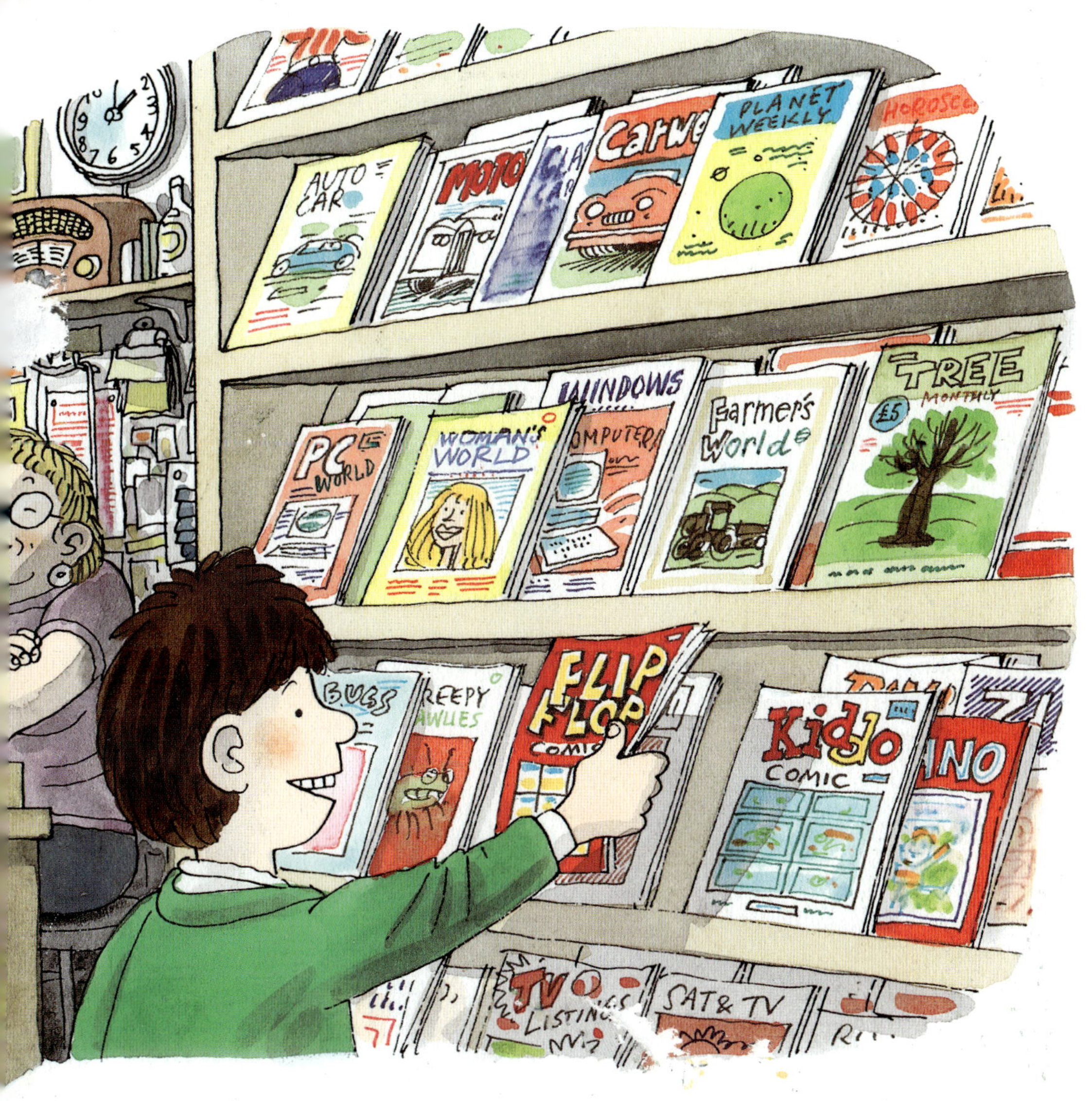

He got a comic.

He went to the market.

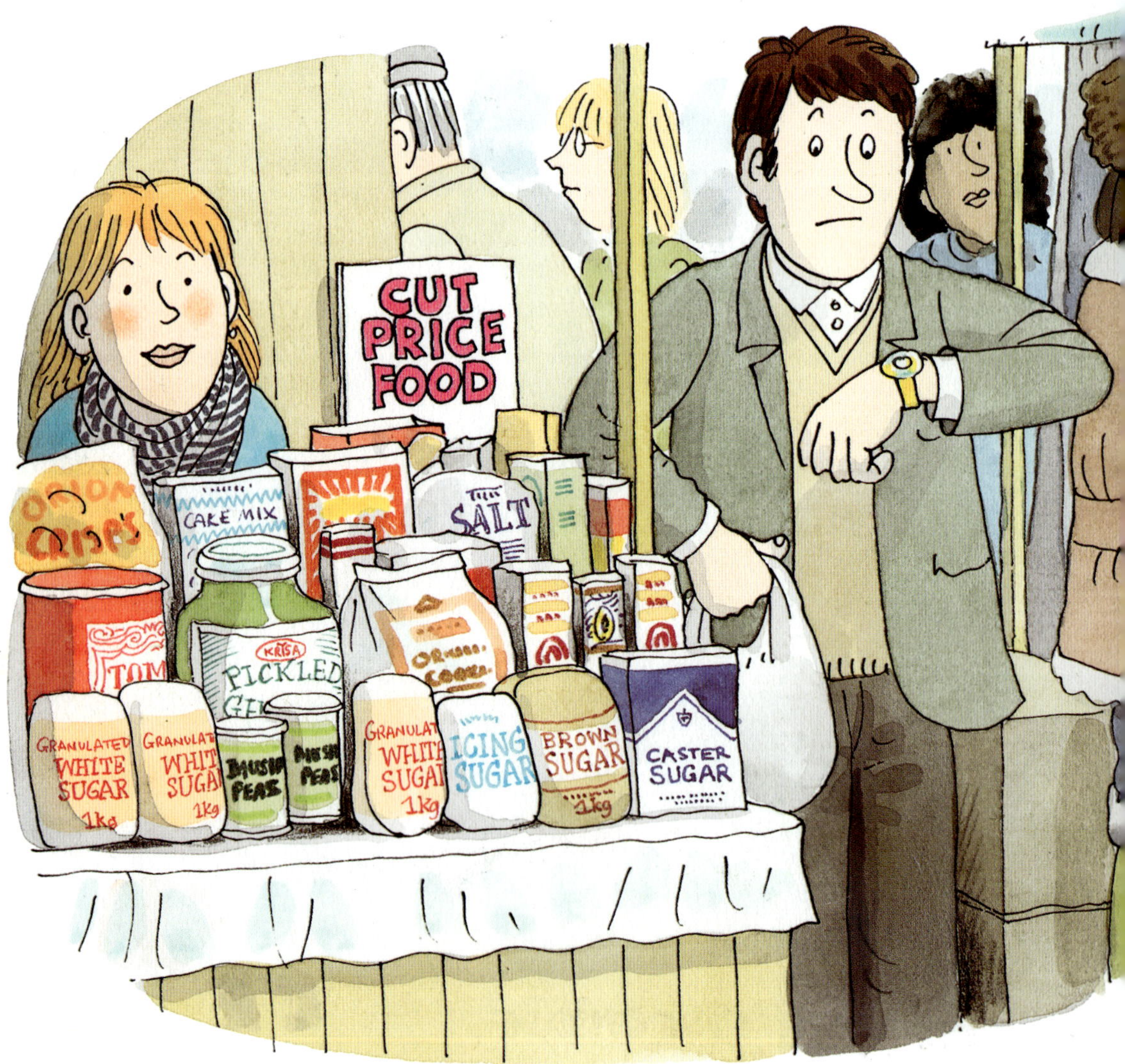

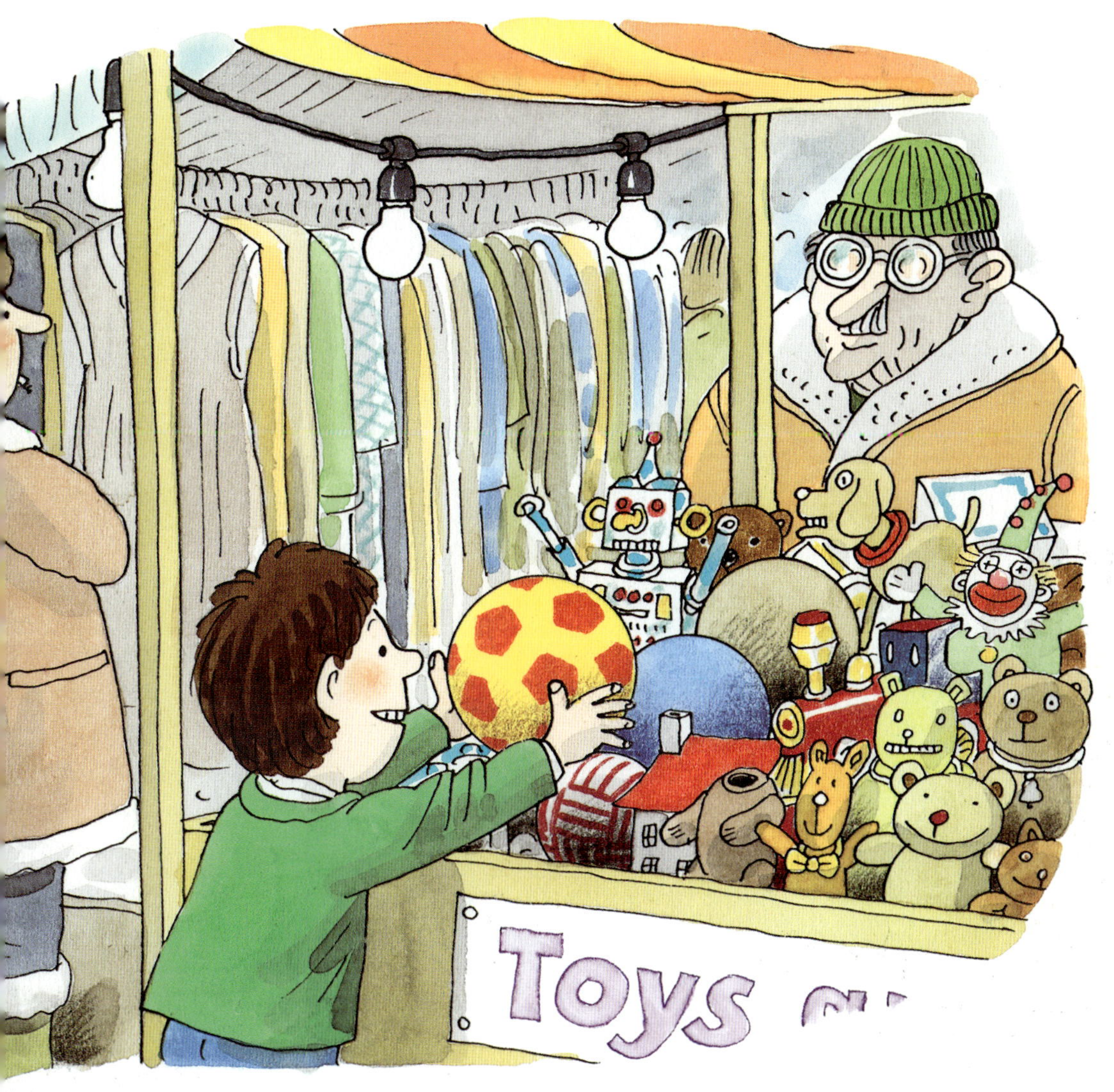

He got a ball.

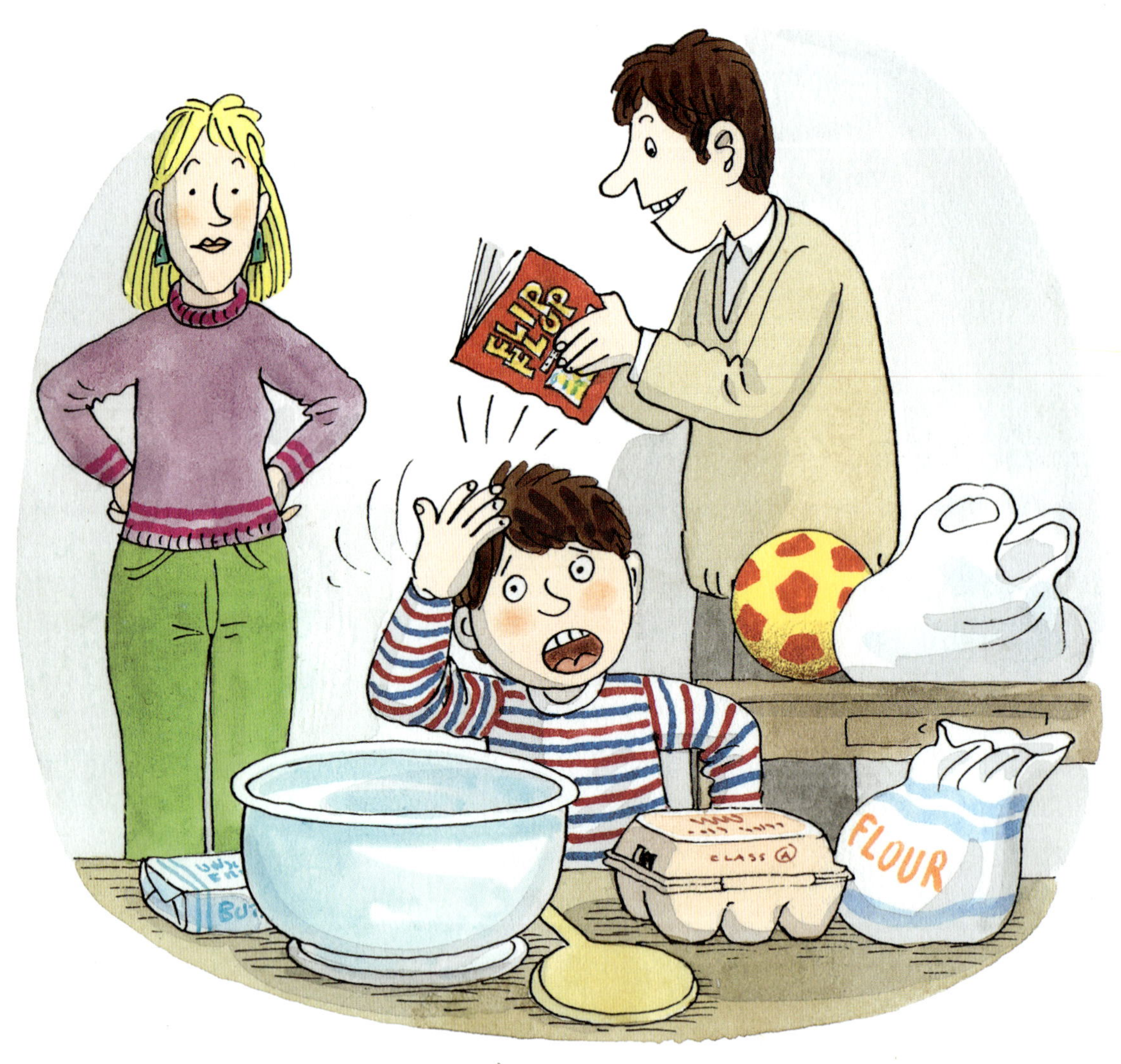

He forgot the sugar.